Nothing Fatal

Akron Series in Poetry

Nothing Fatal

Sarah Perrier

The University of Akron Press
Akron, Ohio

14 13 12 11 10 5 4 3 2 1

LIBRARY OF CONGRESS CATALOGING-IN-PUBLICATION DATA

Perrier, Sarah, 1973–
Nothing fatal / Sarah Perrier.
p. cm. — (Akron series in poetry)
Includes bibliographical references.
ISBN 978-1-931968-87-4 (pbk. : alk. paper) — ISBN 978-1-931968-89-8 (cloth : alk. paper)
I. Title.
PS3616.E77N68 2010
811'.6—DC22
2010012961

The paper used in this publication meets the minimum requirements of American National Standard for Information Sciences—Permanence of Paper for Printed Library Materials, ANSI Z39.48–1984. ∞

Grateful acknowledgment is made to the editors and readers at the following journals where some of the poems included in this manuscript also appeared, sometimes in different versions.
Barn Owl Review: "Too Darn Hot"; *Bat City Review:* "The Apprenticeship" and "Poor Bête Noire"; *Born Magazine:* "Aubade: Easy Mistake"; *The Cimarron Review:* "Ass," "Meeting You: A Definitive Plan," and "Porch with No Swing"; *Cincinnati Review:* "The Queen of Snakes"; *The Cream City Review:* "Patience" and "The Dog, the Yard, the Water, the Problem" (as "The Empathy Kit: How to Be Eight"); *The GSU Review:* "Notes on First Kisses" (as "The Empathy Kit: Notes on First Kisses"); *Hotel Amerika:* "Aubade: Easy Mistake" and "In the Manner of Folklore"; *The Journal:* "My Fortress of Solitude"; *Lake Effect:* "Dark Ride" (as "A Version of the Ark"); *The Ledge:* "How Not to Sleep Around"; *Mid-American Review:* "Rattle Bones"; *New Orleans Review:* "Lesser Beasts"; *North American Review:* "By the Time This Poem Is Over" and "Sexy French Underwear"; *Pebble Lake Review:* "The Empty Seat"; *Phoebe:* "Fresh"; *Pleiades: A Journal of New Writing:* "Near Misses"; *Poemeleon:* "Carnivalesque"; *POOL*: "Poem in Which I Fail to Appear"; *Redactions:* "Domestic Bliss"; *River Oak Review:* "Translation"; *Sou'wester:* "Listless"; and *The Sow's Ear Poetry Review:* "Wanted."
"Pitch the Woo" was selected for inclusion in *Best New Poets 2007*.
Some of these poems have also previously appeared in a chapbook, *Just One of Those Things*, published by Kent State University Press's Wick Poetry Chapbook Series.

Cover: Illustration and cover design by Amanda Gilliland. Type is set in Kuenstler Script.
Nothing Fatal was designed and typeset by Amanda Gilliland. The text was set in News Gothic with headlines in Janson Text. *Nothing Fatal* was printed on 60# Natural and bound by BookMasters of Ashland, Ohio.

Contents

Make me happy, and I shall again be virtuous.

—Frankenstein, *Mary Shelley*

Meeting You: A Definitive Plan

I will not buy two goldfish and name them both Elizabeth Taylor
because there is no telling them apart. I will not decide
they are both Scorpios simply because I am, and because I think
they are mysterious for their distracted way of pouting
around their bowl, turning the curves smoother
each time. Their wet world will not tip like a steaming teapot
into a cup. No cat will lap up its tragic good fortune.
You will not sell me two new fish at a dollar apiece
plus ten more for a new bowl to replace the one gravity got,
and you will not miscalculate the sales tax, and I will not
not get my change back. Chances are, you will not even work
at Bud's Sea and Sky Shop. So in case that's you shopping
the family planning aisle out of wedlock, don't
let our white-haired family pharmacist
with the spooky, walleyed stare catch me smirking
as he assures the woman (who I pray is not your girlfriend)
all the merchandise is "fresh." And since you probably aren't
her supportive older brother checking the date on every box
of every brand, don't think to think about some grand plan
passing you by. Tonight I am as simple as the world's last love poem:
I pay for multivitamins, shoplift a pack of Freshen-Up, leave
the door behind me swinging in front of you.

Porch with No Swing

—after Edward Hopper's Summer Evening

Her clothes are more bare
than the light, and I am sure
the young man is glad.
Late, on a porch with no swing,
his request seems more daring.

He'd like to taste her,
but she's a ripe slice of sour
fruit, pucker and frown
set as the breezeless curtains:
she still hasn't caught his drift.

Her clothes are more bare
than the light. Her lean body
planks against the rail.
With one hand, he asks again.
He still hasn't caught her drift.

Poem in Which I Fail to Appear

I'm not in there, or if I am you cannot see me. I'm hidden
behind the cowboy whose swagger suggests he's all hat,
no cattle. The boozy banker in the brown pinstripe

has taken my chair, and the server has swept away all trace
of the glass I sipped my whiskey from. Look for me pinned
beneath the bar-chord callused hands of some young thing

or in the single stray hair knotted through his rough, shadowed
attitude—a two-day beard and the unlit cigarette he blames
for his stagy smokers' growl. Ask him where he found me,

or try to remember yourself where you lost the last lover
you found—under your thumb, behind your back, back together
again with the cook who kept the kitchen hotly ticking. Send

a waitress to check under the stall doors in the Ladies', keep
one eye on the lonely curb-parked cabbie who closed his book
and winked when you jumped at the flash of his FOR HIRE sign.

Catch him if you can. Look for me on his last dog-eared page.
Then you'll see what happened and when. He did what I said;
I slipped away while he read, and now I am gone, baby, gone.

In the Manner of Folklore

Take a milkweed tea twice yearly to prevent the onset of anything
you're better off without, though more often is best for rickets,

weedy gardens, or children. Stroke a cat's fur backward and see
if sparks rise in the shape of lost loved ones. Fleas cannot be helped,

though some claim their bites add heat when love begins to cool and can
urge the cows to breed, come spring. Don't be cruel with the potatoes

you bury beside the raspberry bramble, even if the neighbor's dog is sure
to dig them up. Don't curse your cure or those warts will grow back twice

the size and black to boot. Unmarried women, as a point of etiquette,
please don't snuff a stranger's candle, or handle an axe blade, even in gloves.

Carry your wits in whatever basket you have, and if a man asks, tell him
you have been hunting for simples. An itch will tell you what you have found.

The Dog, the Yard, the Water, the Problem

Imagine that you and your dog are in the front yard.
The dog must be wet and possibly has soap still sudsing his fur
because you're eight, and even though I'm telling you
what to do, you're going to get part of it wrong. *Good. Very good.*

Feel the sharp small slap of the dog's wet tail against your thigh.
Accidentally spill half the bucket of water you're carrying
on yourself. Miss the dog entirely with the other half of the water.
Now hesitate, as if you are trying to figure out what to do next.

You are trying to be helpful—and that's good—but now you must
stop helping for a moment. Your dog is shaking himself off. His head
and body seem to twist in opposite directions at the same time.
Now your dog is tossing himself in the grass, sending loose blades

into the air. His tail and paws fly upward like a seizure.
You would like to try this, I know. You have watched your parents
practice this at night in their bed. Go ahead, you're eight
and you are eager to grow up. Notice how damp the lawn is.

Remember to make soft snuffling sounds. Wait for your mother.
(Think how she must be about a million years old in dog years.) Wait
for her to bang the door open by throwing her hip against the latch
while kicking the sticking spot loose. She never spills a drop

of her drink. Get up from the grass and tell her you are sorry.
Actually *be sorry* at this point. As sorry as you were last night,
awakened by strange sounds then slapped for being a snoop.
Consider again the growing list of your own shortcomings.

Dance in Two Parts

i.

My moves move like jokes
at cocktail parties, like ice
off a glacier's face.

Tonight I'll wow you
with broken haikus, the dropped
syllables filled in

by flickering stares
or with a flutter of sleeve,
a fan of eyelash—

bless this semaphore
the body flashes. My blush
and hitched, nervous breath

telegraph feelings
in dots and dashes. Words soak
in the tonicked gin

and love might just run
a little smoother for it.
All over the room

sloppy lines knocked out
one too many times fall down
punch-drunk, past clever.

ii.

Don't you feel the sting
of my smile down to your thighs?
I'll give you reason

to press your creases
against mine; ironed and oiled
we steam ahead, mouths

open. Our bodies
release their separate shapes.
Grown cloven, we dance—

a wicked hoof raked
through the grit and hair that sticks
to our joyous skins.

The Queen of Snakes

She must have slithered straight from the root
of a cypress tree. No turner could work his lathe

to cut her jeans' finely fringed cuffs. She rises
from the cracks and mud at the bus stop

like the Queen of Snakes rising from a black knot
of reptile hide. She never watches her step. The snakes

climb higher, wrapping their fat bodies
around the slim joint of her ankle so tightly

they could snap it with a careless twitch. They twist
their bodies into a wriggling braid, they slide

over one another, knowing only the pleasure of skin
touching skin. She feels nothing for her minion,

yet he dreams of his hands drawing up slipknots
of her hair. She takes a slow drag of clove smoke,

wet winter turns a little more exotic for a block
in either direction. Then a flick of ash. Openmouthed,

he breathes in her scent and taste, his tongue
stabbed clean through with a silver stud.

Rattle Bones

In the lab the mad doctors stitch up the seams that will never heal into scars. Their monster, they know, will be all jigsaw puzzle and skin graft, but they love the craziness of their quilt. Each night a different one sleeps on the slab tucked beside the cold mass of their genius.

Come morning, they pull on their lab coats—worn mostly for looks and for warmth—knowing there is work to be done. Today's question: where will they put the soul? On this debate the sides seem evenly split: half heart, half brain. A few rogues point lower.

Wrapped in their white coats and gloves, they frown over their progress. One thinks the monster looks a little like him. He blushes with pride when his boss praises the careful way he has chosen each toe; he had hoped his attention to detail would not go unnoticed.

Flexing the left foot again, he checks the tension rising in the line of the Achilles tendon, the loft of the sculpted arch, all along dreaming he will be the one to whisper into their lovely monster's ear and rattle those three delicate bones for the first time. *Speak,* he will say, *tell them you're alive.*

How Not to Sleep Around

Cats call out their crazy love,
and the amphitheater alley bellows back
their lunatic heat. The creek bed cuts
corners, and its shale banks sag like furniture.
Familiar sheets twist against your own
unmixed sweat. In the other world, lovers carry on,
and someone clutches you like a handbag
in a bad part of town. Someone hollers,
Keep it down! and summer settles in
while you name its every sound, name the heat
that swells in cycles and waves you on
toward that one last thing you're waiting
to feel: either cooler nights and quiet sleep,
or a hotter way to cool your heels.

Poor Bête Noire

I dream of days I used to bask in vats of tears. I made
every morsel—every scrap of bone—I spat a finger
I licked clean of someone dear. Now at best
I cheat a tip, resist glad wishes for a good new year.
Gone are days I ran with the gas man, the tax man,
the grocer who skimped, his thumb always on the scale.
Instead I prowl a town that howls itself to sleep, no better
than a kennel. What use are my thoughts of plunder
when every victim's gone reform? Every road I ruin
leads to the same small town stuffed with knives
and books of matches set to spark a dangerous torch.
The whole town's barking now, and still no one asks me
or my fleas to leave. We're made proper, civilized
right down to these first wondrous, wretched tears.

Aubade: Easy Mistake

No wonder the sun rose and soaked my bed in watery light
better suited to laundry than to love. No wonder dawn
dragged itself up into a full gray sky. I strip the sheets,

and the washer swishes its hips at the first touch
of a button. The coffee maker drips too slowly
to enjoy such a rushing ruckus, but the manufacture

of some fast hot heat is not a mystery to everything
in the kitchen: the tea kettle fairly squeals each time
the microwave completes its calisthenics routine.

Beauty and strength—both are lost on the wobbly fan
that totters all night long like a drunken chanteuse,
more the idea-of-cool than cool itself. Easy, I suppose,

to mistake its cheap squeak for morning birds coming on
two dim hours before the forty-watt sun at last laid bare
the forsythia without its yellow, the world its wonder.

Listless

Let the lioness lie, sleepy, in the shade of one bare tree
and dream of small puddles, so the drought may seem less
long. And a dream, too, for the baboon, who doesn't see
the lion slip her tongue in one dry loop across her teeth. A flight

of featherless wings, wasps and bats like nightmares diving
from rooftops to the open spaces below, streaks the sunset
with a thousand reasons to panic at the sky's unlined
lanes of traffic. Every set of wings strong-arms the evening

into pairs of hungers, pairs of thirsts. Closer, one hand draws
its sustenance from the one body it knows best. The moon
is inconvenient, it reeks like a stale tooth—the root's gone
rotten, there's nothing to be done. All that heavenly ether

only helps the ache burn brighter. Now, here a candle,
here a window, a warped wood door that won't close true.
A wick that smolders, an oiled hinge, and that breath—
almost a word—when the hungry world at last lies quiet.

Sexy French Underwear

is sexy, so I shimmy on my *sous-vêtements* each morning,
though the tatty lace, machine washed too often to pass

as *lingerie*, sags, inelastic. At least I try, I tell myself—though I keep
quieter than Victoria's Secret about the time I went bust

in a twice-worn *bustier*. Does my French pay off?
When I feed the cat, do you purr, imagining canary feathers

tickling the backs of my thighs? When I drive my car
(God, yes, the *Citroën*!) do you go wild around my curves?

I hum *La Marseillaise* as we come, I cry for *Liberté*
and all the rest of it, but sirens wail in fourths, and, *c'est dommage,*

every ribbon, every accent comes out wrong: I say *merci,*
though I mean something like pity. You say *de rien*

as if kindness were a little piece of nothing. We wear
each other down this way, a *négligée*, the slip or the savor

of a foreign tongue. The thinnest of understandings flutters
between us. I simmer—a dark roast, a thick soup—I'm French

like nobody's business. Who knows if you love me for *les bras*,
for my brain, for my *softassnow*? Who cares? You read me wrong again.

My Fortress of Solitude

I want to wear him like the snap-brim hat that keeps
Clark Kent's sleek blue-streaked hairdo greased
into pomade's most perfect expression of strength
and hold. I want so much control the disguise

leaves crowds of anxious bystanders blown away
by my hidden life, the impossibility of such a singular
double nature. I want to be seen here, overlooked
over there in my work clothes, somehow too daily for even this,

the dailiest of planets. Let me wear him
down until he's become my most comfortable shoes,
my shabby hat and threadbare coat, the house
where I alone can live and where I can live a little

less alone. He'll hold me close until we can fly
further south into those Antarctic climes
where even predators cannot take the harsh winter
wind that blows survival away and solitude shelters us

in its crystalline architecture. We'll poke around
in exotic furs and layers of socks, warming ourselves
against the chill that comes through the walls, even in summer.
I'll leave Paris and all of Italy to lovers who need good light

or heat to find each other beautiful. Give me instead the cold
slip and thrust of Krypton's massive faults, the sweep
of a clean glacial field to prove our isolation amid winds
that chap our skins to burlap, rubbed too sore to touch.

Augury: Haiku at the Dragon Wok

A hint of almond
or lemon gone stale; the taste
of the folded moon.

The plastic wrapper
crackles with Earthly Delights.
One must always choose.

Break it and let crumbs
rain down on jade palaces
captured in red ink

or tell me, sweet thing,
you don't believe in desserts.
See where that gets you.

Notes on First Kisses

Allen Wexler thought he was the first, and I let him
strut that fact for days. The only myth of first kisses

is that there is only one. The first kiss on the lips,
the first one with tongues. The first with feeling

(it's probably fear). How can you believe
a word I say, once you know where my mouth

has been? Josh Elias asked first. Kenny Hudgins
should have brushed his teeth better. Can you

believe a word I say, until you know what else
my mouth can do? Shut up and kiss me, fool.

Too Darn Hot

Why sort the doubletalk from the innuendo?
They're both lyrical. Two secrets
linger between us, though one is a lie

I'll tell to keep the other company, but still
I can't make you disappear with ease—
no penny beneath my palm, no token to stitch

inside the seam of tonight's star-striped suit.
Silvery and besotted, the mayflies swat us
for our bad behavior—the heat's a strap,

the moon its buckle. I can't bother to pour you
a glass of whiskey straight from a bottle cast
in glass so green even money sickens

with envy—you might enjoy it. I've given up
drinking even the de-loveliest wine. What's left,
beside the banter and the boredom, a script

so stale there's no telling what it means to anyone?
Risks should whistle with possibility, but why woo
a man I don't like enough even to hum? I'd prefer

a Cole Porter tune—something a little more upright,
a little more grand. Nothing now but a yawn for you,
one last thank you—*thank you*—and good night.

Lesser Beasts

Bare-handed, I snapped all the necks
on a six-snouted pig named Lucius
and beat back Lycoris, the bringer

of dull evenings. Now come, lesser beasts,
imps and sprites, swarms of you
like gnats in the yard. Here's a saucer

of vinegar to lap, a small bowl of cloves
to fatten up on before I pluck you
from your own burpy stupor. The staccato

gallops of the night-mares' hooves will slur
and thicken in the strip of honey I've spread
on the windowsill; their hollow bones will keep

until I sift them from the black ants' trails.
I'll blow their dust back to the distant north,
shine their saddles like trophies to hang

from my jacket buttons. Beware my open hand,
beware my wicked tongue—it cleans my teeth
like a plague cleans a field. It's the gristle

that causes the glint, gorgeous prey. Rattle
your chest full of coins against my knuckles
while I split your ribs. My fingers fly along

your bent spine, it tends toward the bowstring
of my will. And listen—our song—
my breath in your mouth, your last note.

Carnivalesque

Bargains were struck. Firemen dressed as clowns, Jaycees' Wives made snow cones, and the Chamber of Commerce sold raffle tickets. Andrea Nelson wore perfume and stole a hanky from her father's drawer. Everywhere we turned, there were gimmicks and traditions.

The half-formed catechism of the carnival repeated in every flashing bulb along the fairway, and we circled its raw boards and straw as the devoted walk the floors of Chartres.

He kissed with one eye open. *What does this mean?*

He asked to dip my hair in grease. *What does this mean?*

Mothers wept. Fathers blinked. The brass band clanged away.

Then the Ferris wheel came down and the fun house folded up—it turned out to be a trailer home painted, gutted, and rewired. The whole town buzzed and blared. Blame had to be misplaced. *What does this mean?* Some sentences began "My daughter. . . ." Some began "Those carnies."

Fresh

When Kevin Miller's mother called me *fresh*
before swaying up her driveway, I didn't know
her New Jersey twang was from New Jersey

or that when she called me
fresh she meant to make me
sorrier than her son was for the game

he started with kisses. I ran after him
until his wrist was fast in my grip
and his belly was flat in the dirt. The soft

pop of his skin beneath my teeth
is still as fresh as the sting in my mouth
where I stretched it sore at the corners.

His mother stopped in her tracks when I spat
the missing bit of his dirty cotton shirt at her heels,
and she spat back with *fresh*. Suppose his response

had been that sharp. Suppose my kneecaps
hadn't cracked two of his twiggy ribs
and left him forgetting how to handle

his next breath. Suppose he had been
heels-dug-in stubborn and refused to run.
The messages our bodies send us

and deliver us from—quick as currents
running to ground—snap and arc
under the force of our telling (the synapse

filters flash, and the story is recast):
If he hadn't run away, he could have won.
And now if the knot of his scar could untie itself

and slip back into skin, it would only be
one more thing he left behind
when I watched his mother load half

a houseful of her, her wisdom
and her furniture, onto a truck
and head back to New Jersey.

Before he began, the dentist shook
his thumb over his right shoulder, asked me
if I "wanted one like that." Kevin Miller

was long gone, and my trophy—my chipped
incisor—was filed smooth. By summer, I learned
to throw out a hip and carry a comb.

I hung out at the corner of Rollerskate
and Ten Speed with a pack of cigarettes
I knew how to light but couldn't yet

smoke. On the corner
we played "Truth" and let
the good lies slide until Nicole

Ryan dared Steve Swisher to a game,
then fired off a pack of lies.
Had she, or would she ever? *Yeah.*

With a boy? *Yeah.* With Brian
Wilburne? *We were gonna but*
he just had his braces tightened.

With a girl? *No way, Steve.*
You're the only queer I know.
And none of us said a word.

Then Megan, who knew about sins
of omission, heard her mother call, and Ruth,
who always played by the rules, said it was hers.

Then Ben and Adam Morgan rode off
without a word. Nicole spat out her gum,
said, *Let's don't tell, right? We don't*

ever tell. When he asked me if I wanted
one like that, I wondered if the dentist meant the girl
or her thousand dollar smile.

Did I really have to choose? Could I
tell him anything without a word
like *complicit?*

♡

We still don't tell. None of us would ever
say a word about how Nicole
was easier than a boy, or mention

how she let us kiss her, so long
as we kept our eyes open
and did what she told us to do:

No. The boy puts his hands here.
The trouble with secrets is keeping them
quiet enough. Is choosing who

to tell each story to. Nicole never told
anyone who didn't already know, and I
never told anyone at all. I lied to Allen

Wexler through my straightened teeth,
said it just came natural, because maybe it did
for someone. In the woods, behind the traffic rails

at the dead ends of streets; in basements
and bedrooms and borrowed cars;
in the alley behind the drugstore;

and under the bleachers at away games,
the difference between postulate
and theorem was made manifest

on a familiar scale, without a reminder
that failures have always been
part of the proof. The exclusive properties

of either *saving myself* or *giving it out*
on the cheap seemed less exclusive
the night Rob McKerney kicked me out

of his car for not wanting to go all the way.
He had said we would just *practice*, but Rob
didn't want to practice like Nicole and I had.

I hadn't considered not believing him
when he said we wouldn't do it in his car.
Whichever way, the story is the same.

I can only allow for so much discretion,
and if my stories seem to hedge their bets,
it's a habit I've picked up with experience:

John Ackerman pulled my hand to his crotch
during an assembly. What if I had
pulled away instead of trying

to imitate what I told Rob McKerney I wouldn't do?
Then John Ackerman wouldn't have held
his books low as he left the auditorium,

and I wouldn't have wondered what John
Ackerman's mother said when she found
those jeans in the wash. Then I wouldn't

have said yes when Theresa Vincente
asked, *That's it? That's all it is?*
She expected stories of hands

under my shirt and voices dropping
to soft guttural gasps. Not the simple
synchronous looks away. Not quiet

disavowals and throat-clearings without even,
simply, a thank you. The whole truth
is only part of the story—the skin

over the flesh and bone of experience.
I have let what comes firsthand
come first. Everything else resists

translation into narrative—the story doesn't end.
There is no moment I can point to, say
This is when things changed. Kevin Miller,

I'd still pin you down in the dirt,
if only to tell your mother to take back
the time she called me *fresh;* if only

to ask Nicole Ryan if what happened
happened only to me. If only to say
none of this happened only to my body.

On the Principle of Pairing in Nature

Still-single friends fill you with logic: If you want to hunt big game, they will say, you must find it where it lives. Want a lion? Get thee to the dark continent of love where prides of doctors and lawyers run free through happy hours, nightclubs, and upscale retail centers. If you point out that you could be a gazelle, and that could be bad, they will repeat their advice, as if it's you who didn't get the point.

And for the arty type, order pizza, they say. The musician willing to starve for his art delivers. The painter delivers. The sculptor, performance artist, struggling first novelist, aspiring actor/director, documentary filmmaker, and songwriter all deliver. Call. Wait. He will come to you fresh, hot, and in thirty minutes or less. He will come guaranteed.

If you are too hungry to wait, go to the drive-thru. Look at the speaker, speak directly to it. You will hear a promise of love so rich you'll devour it, want more. You'll want to circle the parking lot again and again just to hear the voice promise he'll "bewitch you in a moment."

Take classes at the community center, they say. Even the ones that don't interest you. Yogacize. Learn to look in every crowd for someone dressed like your soul mate. Always look alert and receptive. Dress like someone else's soul mate. Most of all, don't look like you're looking. But don't look and—*poof!*—you disappear.

Dark Ride

In the penny arcade, the player piano jukes and nickel slots
warm for the Big Winner ready to take the money

and run away to some tropical island a little less cloudy
than heaven, or perhaps head someplace dimmer,

where blinding ether doesn't boil all vision to a bubbling glare.
Soon, someone will unscrew the half-shot midway bulbs

from their rusty sockets, strike the duck pond's flume,
its herd of plastic quackers numbered and dumb

as the nervous pairs adrift in the swan-shaped boats
that bump along the Laugh-in-the-Dark. But first,

two by two, they sail, they *s'amuser* with a little covert clutch
and rub, they feel brave when the waters do not rise. At last

these tame and timid creatures pushed their luck—
nothing's fatal—everything's wild, nothing beats their pair.

The Apprenticeship

It started so romantic, the night he hauled her empty head
and all the rest to sea, her skirt blooming like a calico jellyfish

dandling its tentacles across her thighs. He whispered
as he rowed: *blossom, stroke.* Each vowel and breath foretold
a kiss he wished to press against her saltless flesh. Also in the boat,

a sack of scraps: six flawed earlobes, the several knees
that would not grow weak in close proximity to flowers,

and the brain, wobbling like a cake on a plate beneath the bell jar's
fragile skull. In a rowboat, what praise or nicknames were his
to use? His dizzy feelings grew faint each time the harbor's chop

cracked his shoulder bones. He had observed the calibration
of her body, had helped, in fact, contrive the swoop of bone

above her hips—where he had held the rope, his palms still pricked
with phantom splinters, their constant itch a portent of the fatal shift:
he left docile study for a thrill he felt as a note drawn from his chest,

though his swelling panic nixed the note's vibrato; he knew the gesture
of his rowing wouldn't stop the stars going skew. They often do.

Water Speaks to Our Subconscious Selves

The power was out, so the TV wouldn't work and the garage door was stuck shut. Everyone stayed in. No moths' wings opened or closed in the darkness above the front door. *Tip: Drink half a glass of water before bed. Remembering your dreams is as easy as drinking the other half when you wake up.*

I couldn't tell if anyone ever stepped out on anyone else. All along, when other parents were running around, I figured mine were busy doing something different. I mean, I guessed they must have been. I went to bed early. A whole lake froze, and its shale cliffs eroded.

Trouble was they never said how big a glass. And by morning, you'd think they'd have come back on, the lights. I was so thirsty my voice cracked for good. I still can't remember if they were in color, what I looked like, or if I could fly.

Academic Affairs

Why don't you love me, and we can hit the road together,
cruise the lecture circuit and tell other people

about the work it takes to make it work. Together,
we'll talk talk talk about the necessity of long-term

memory and the value of the grudge. Your flipchart
of my body parceled out like a butcher's map

shows the exact locations of too much and too little
with tiny stuck-on arrows, their sharp points as fine

as my revenge: reading poems instead of lectures,
each one a reminder of other men I left for doing less.

Afterward, alone again, come up beside me, nuzzle my ear
and quote Foucault: *Tomorrow, sex will be good again.*

Now add, *But tonight you're on your own.* This is how
itinerant scholars of loss communicate: quote, footnote—

our endnotes and marginalia are full of longing for the pet
projects we can't let go, yours on fixing up my life, mine

a love poem I've been working on for years. It reads,
I can take it if you can; I can take it if you can.

Sweet Nothings

You're my little blossom, Buttercup. My sweet
butter pat to spread across the sheets' unwholesome
slice of goodness. Let's not let the literalists make love

harder by asking that we must mean so precisely
what we say. Indulge my weakness for the rotten
rhetoric that covers up the scratched tracks

you stalk, Tiger. See how I pounce on the chance
to satisfy my sweet tooth for words, my sticky need
to keep you sedate, dazed in a half-baked, sugared state?

Let me call you Sweetheart to keep you only as close
as the shopkeepers who call me Honey. Baby, you know
our business has been more than good. I won't burn

with a figurative flame unless your sweetness melts
in a word. Sugar, dissolve in my mouth or crumble
and let me call you my Cookie, my Muffin, my Ruin.

By the Time This Poem Is Over

some readers will wish the genre of the love poem were more popular
because someone will hurt someone else in line eight. The reader's eyes

will have giddyupped across two little lies and a big, juicy whopper
there's no hope of catching. The tides will have shifted and displaced

the sand that marks their margins; we will move closer
to the second ice age when that sand will grind canyon lips

down into deepest bedrock. A bed will stop rocking beneath two lovers
who neither love nor need each other (the poem will end

with their starting up again). When it's over, it's over or it's not,
but tell that to the painter who claimed he finished painting the same way

he finished making love. I guess having sweat through some fabrics
he changed the canvas as a housewife might change the sheets

after her lover leaves. (What a racket those two made!) By the time
this poem is over, that quilt will be awash in sweat and dander, shadows

steeped in a swelter so sultry one of us will feel like lighting up—
didn't their love make you think of words like *smolder*? By now

it is almost time for us to leave each other, but first let me ask you,
what's your name, my love? You look like someone I used to write about.

Near Misses

Forget about the fat angel and his sack of arrows; tipped up
on one chubby foot, he always seems to be falling. Flipped up

on edge, the pool rafts bask in the sun and the concrete sweats
beads of water. Everyone's schedule is just a bit off-kilter, ripped up

by holidays and interruptions. By Monday morning the glad,
grabbing lovers who ached for flesh the day before will have zipped up

and down the elaborately turning paths of the public gardens
so thoroughly every witness will know the pair is tripped up

by each other's still being there. There is an intimate stink
like the magnolia's woozy rot, those tacky flowers, so open-lipped. Up

early, out of habit, they don't kiss. One yawns, one shakes
or scratches. The fat angel takes his aim. Breakfast gets whipped up.

It's a hit! The Perrier bottle's green curve goes to pieces, its insides
begin to love the floor. The tile is slick. Someone's slipped up.

Welcome

to the city built once upon a time. You've been waiting
for the freeze-frame, the flashing, slow-motion moment

to arrive—angels' bells and drumrolls thrumming—
and, good citizen, you did not miss it. You've learned

five kinds of love in three languages, and so we share
a common tongue. Here you can have your best

first kiss, over there, a lengthy goodbye (by the stairs
where fortune-tellers lurk, but never lie). Shall we lean

together, posed like mannequins, our arms
around each other's waists, proclaim our love beyond

the force of body, mind, or habit? We have it
on good authority that this is fate—forecast

down to the weather and propitious date. Hand
in hand before the broken sign for RTIFICIAL LIMBS,

we stand, written in according to plan. We'll kiss—
by the next line you'll love me. Three later, I'll leave.

Domestic Bliss

I'll tell you what it's like, my married friend says. *It's always dark*
where he's from. She lives in an unknown country: the walls rise
slick and lemony from bright tile floors, the tabletops taste
like vitamin C. In her kitchen, the knife blades break their teeth

on her fear. She won't look. Once, she dared me to curse
the dark mirror in her bathroom. She promised to save my soul
with a flick of a switch. Now it comes to this: parts of chickens
in her garbage can, loads of dark clothes to scrub. She tells me

about the bathroom scale, about the kitchen sink. She's afraid
the shower curtain might snap into a wall of fire. Even now,
she hears its dangerous flapping down the hall. *Stand right there,*
she says, and cuts the lights. *Where he's from, all the stairs point down.*

Texas

It didn't much matter anymore if he was a bullfighter, a cattle roper, or a rodeo clown. You wanted to feel callused hands, watch them run smooth along the fence rails. His palms would almost shine, daring the wood to splinter.

In Clear Spring there's nothing but a field full of trucks and the Clear Spring Saloon, but you were still singing about the Terlingua—not thinking of Waylon or Willie, but mainly of the boys. I told you to buckle up.

But *Sweet God* how you saw them! Rowdy, cocksure, and lovely in their swaggers. You'd kiss them hard just to prove their lips could bruise. In Seguin someone asked us what two girls from way up North were doing in Texas. You said you were down here looking for the whole enchilada.

Rodeo isn't the same thing as *The Rodeo,* and neither of us knew that leaving Chicago. Not cows, *cattle,* they told us. Halfway out of Austin we stopped counting tumbleweeds and cows. When I asked for directions to The Rodeo at a gas station in Luckenbach they told me, *It's in February.*

Translation

—a lament for Emperor Wu of the Han and his concubine

Suppose it was her meatloaf he loved
and that they had made plans to buy her a color TV
as soon as they could. Suppose he loved her

unreasonably, with the feverish intensity of a sailor
who's been out to sea too long. That in their kisses
this woman could run her hand across the thick knot

of his salted beard, then knuckle her fear to his chest
and throat until it choked him as wisteria vines might
topple such strength—with sweetness, color, and musk.

Or with his grief, give him youth and anger,
a pack of cigarettes, a waitress to ask what he wants.
To be the king of nothing, perhaps, or else to make a study

of the hours, of the wristwatch and the water clock,
to unwind the days until his grief no longer runs
clockwise, and no longer at the slow second hand's pace.

Ass

Sure, my ex tells me, *you can say "ass"*
with anything. For emphasis especially.

Like the word is the white blouse my mother said went
with everything. The black patent leather

shoes that dress up any outfit, but don't really
reflect up. It just doesn't seem like a compliment

to say a woman has a "fun ass sense of humor."
The conversation is going nowhere, but thank God

it's midsummer so I can play like I swallowed a gnat
because it's believable and I'd rather let my ex

(we're still friendly) feel sorry for me about that.
Let him think I flinched over some bug

he couldn't even see, so he can slap my back
and try to hand me my drink again, the ice cubes

squeaking against the curve of the tumbler as they melt
into the already wet air. *So the dog won't listen,*

he'd cheer at me if he figured out the tiny fly was a fake,
and I'd hear him out, so he wouldn't have to feel

the daily impotence of people who make their livings
watching people cry. Let him think what he likes.

What he likes is the woman in his office
who always wears a black bra and has a tattoo.

(*A teddy bear on the inside of her wrist!*
It's no bigger than a dime! he gushed.)

I think the bug trick might be working.
My ex just says, *Those candles never work,*

do they? and rattles the loose ice in his glass. Citronella
burns through the neighborhood. The dog returns

to its post, a mat of plastic grass near the door,
and snouts around. Animal possessiveness

(we're still friendly) uncocks its ears,
braces for this evening's mosquitoed assault.

Personal Poem

Dear Reader: Be my material! Seeking solution to invention problem. Me: well-versed, strong interest in voice. You: scary uncle meets muse. You: literate, but ill-tempered, reeking of inks and bindings. You: Fickle. You is not me. You turns the page, I goes on—spine-cracked, read-out, shelf-cocked, and foxed—from there.

Proper Care and Feeding

I eat
twice a day. Feed
me a line, I'll follow
the shimmer and glitz of your lure.
Let's switch.

Now you
play the wolf, stare
me down until my flesh
comes right off the bone with just one
yellow

flicker
of your eyes. Try
now to imagine me
as a circling fin; I'm hungry
again—

you'd best
not struggle so.
I'm streamlined, I focus.
I know you so well your body
has scars

I have
yet to cause. Don't
expect us to be less
than wary of ourselves. We bite
back, we

fight. Howl
louder: I crave
your body's racket—deep
and solid as an ache—steady
echo

(echo)
of the fevered
sound my own flesh makes. Plain
as salt behind my snarl, I lie
in wait,

a shriek
in my throat. Wild-
blooded, I feel the thrum
surge with your approach, my sweet prey,
my beast.

Partial Still Life with Ottoman

Fancy with zebra hide, the ottoman flicked
an idle hoof, bumped the dog's wagless surrender

to boredom until it unsnuffled its snout and paws
from their feather of tail and the floors clattered

with castanets of dogclaw, claves of jaw and jowl.
The slurp of a salivary yawn, then everything resettled

beneath the chairs that nosed the table's beveled edge
like a circle of ponies at the trough. The switch flicked

with whip-crack precision, and the jangle of keys, klaxon-
like, wakened the sleeping dust and the musty animal

kingdom retreated unscratched and unloved. Brushed
and thrust aside, a jacket sulked across the chair back,

the acetate satin lining shivering above the windy joint
where a cobweb won't grow. This undone stillness

offers no allegory: no skull bobs on the mantel, ready
to scuttle the sense from my head. What doesn't move

doesn't want to. No undepicted hand waits to stroke
the scene, but here's my hand, full of fidget and animal

fever—a whole barnyard of desire—to tap and stamp
the bare-handed news: to love is to move.

The Empty Seat

—*after* Nighthawks

Because I wished her sadness were less well-dressed
or that her date seemed a little less indifferent,

I left while she read a sugar packet or matchbook
and he smoked, though I'd like to point out

there wasn't an ashtray in sight. He's a cad,
it's clear. She deserves better. In a dress like that

she deserves a driver to whisk her from soirée
to soirée, to hold her coat and stole. Let me

choose from all of Europe's oldest bridges the one
she'll look best on, strolling with me as we dare

the rain to fall on anyone as happy as we are.
Across the empty Atlantic of my unfilled glass,

the waters ebb and nip. The cad can't imagine her crossing
Pont Neuf in spring or the Rialto in red Italian sandals.

Patience

At last, the sound of metal rolled flat
by open places, and then the press
of the whistle muscling through
brambles. The sound of darkness
hunting itself in the backyard

like a streak of pure weight.
On the other side of the tracks
someone fiddles with a radio.
Someone taps one fingernail
on the steering wheel or stands

in a doorway, ready to wish
in case a caboose comes by. Suppose
just once there weren't coal cars
but loads of cut diamonds blaring
their fire straight down

the main line between this world
and the next. Or better still,
a passenger train to bring
the one face you've been waiting for,
with its rumpled brow

and delicate wrists. That skin that asks
to be touched because inch
by inch it is becoming an expanse. Now
say, *Hello,* or *I have always loved this weather,*
or *I have always loved you.*

Wanted

He's the meanest man I've ever seen: declared dangerous
and wanted by the FBI. I love him a little,

mostly for not living on my street. His sketch snarls
at the jittery girl two ahead of me in line. He's ready

to take on anyone who thinks he's tough. *Buster,*
I could tell him, *you don't know from tough.*

Take a look: it's ten past five and the line is long
(the clerk's dinner will be cold again). And the bride

with her romantic sense of stamps that take licking
is stuck here too, her face fixed in place, inelegant

and faintly ill as she double-counts two hundred
ivory laid invitations, each one graced with a satin bow

and bride-licked stamp. The jittery girl is nonplussed
by such nostalgia: her airbrushed acrylic fingernails tap,

tap, tap out *stupid bitch* and her snow boots squeak in agreement.
Bad ideas end up here. The signs say nothing fragile

or stuffed with razor blades, no packages soaked
in butane or sent without a correct return address—

as if anyone ever wants to come back here. The cops drive through
slowly in the afternoons, are never seen after dark.

Fuckitscold shudders the last man in, and the bride and I
and the jittery girl all throw him looks that say, *Manners,*

young man, in glares as glassy as the door bumping shut
behind him. Perhaps he loves someone, has a note that says so

like the bride (though not the clerk whose wife hasn't bothered
to keep a meal warm in fifteen years). Or else he's lonely, he's bored

enough to wonder if he could still get a money order on demand
or else a box with a little key to call his own, a reason

to leave his house each day—to check his rented slot for the note
no one knows how to write or where to send. *Next, please.*

The line shuffles forward, and I move closer
to my mean-eyed love, the stranger last seen shooting up

the swollen heart of a bank vault in Texas. He's the one
who got away—at least according to the sign. *Tell it to the law,*

pal, says the jittery girl's indifference. *No,* I say. *Tell me.* Explain
your hands, dull enough to pull a trigger, to etch the letters

of a lover's name into a fistful of fingernails, engraved
like the bride's every last invitation. I only want

what can be had: a letter and a photograph sent from far away.
A simple meal and then a clean, outrageous escape.

Pitch the Woo

Let's lose it, baby; let's forget
the fever, the flowers, the dinner and dancing,
and all the jazzy lines we throw out for waiters

so they know they can slap that check down
anywhere they please. Give me your heart

on a platter. And look, your lovely, loose fist
opens to show off—like magic—mine. It's smaller
than you thought, and lumpy as unwashed socks.

Let's send romance out for groceries
and a tank of gas. Let's guzzle sweet tea

or warm beer straight from a dented can.
Don't promise a thing until you can look
and see space, not stars. Unstitch every last sequin

from the dress it's been hitched to. Touch
my thigh, say skin is skin, the heart a muscle. Say

your words are nothing but words; I know you
are ready to bore me right through. Now try me.
I want to try you, too.

Notes

Epigraph
This promise is offered as a bargain when the Monster confronts Dr. Frankenstein in order to ask for a mate.

Listless
The word listless is rooted in the Middle English list, meaning appetite or desire. Thus, to be listless is to be without appetite or desire—lustless.

Dark Ride
In the language of the amusement park, a dark ride is a "tunnel of love" or "laugh-in-the-dark" attraction.

Domestic Bliss
"Once, she dared me to curse / the dark mirror in her bathroom. She promised to save my soul / with a flick of a switch." Such promises were made at sleepovers. The idea was to summon the devil by locking yourself in a pitch-black bathroom and chanting, "Hell, Bloody Hell." The switch-flicker was in charge of rescue, should the devil actually appear.

Partial Still Life with Ottoman
The final line owes a debt to Frank O'Hara's "In Memory of My Feelings," though O'Hara's poem offers a slightly different premise: "to move is to love."

To the many friends and colleagues who supported me during the writing of the poems in this book, my best and warmest. In particular, I'd like to thank my teachers, especially Jennifer Atkinson, Don Bogen, John Drury, Joanie Mackowski, and Eric Pankey, who helped me trust the work of writing poems. Thanks, too, to Bob Murdock and Joan Houlihan, Jeffrey Levine, and Ellen Doré Watson from the Colrain Poetry Manuscript Conference, whose insights helped renew my enthusiasm and care along the way. For their patience, dedication, and support in the production of this book, Mary Biddinger, Amy Freels, Amanda Gilliland, and everyone else at University of Akron Press, I cannot say thank you enough. Likewise, Maggie Anderson and the Wick Poetry Chapbook Series, Nin Andrews, Matthew Guenette, and Dora Malech have my thanks. And for my family, whose warmth, wisdom, trust, insight, enthusiasm, care, patience, and dedication have exceeded all of these, my love and gratitude that I carry with me everywhere—like ink under my skin.

Akron Series in Poetry

Mary Biddinger, Editor

Sarah Perrier, *Nothing Fatal*
Oliver de la Paz, *Requiem for the Orchard*
Rachel Dilworth, *The Wild Rose Asylum*
John Minczeski, *A Letter to Serafin*
John Gallaher, *Map of the Folded World*
Heather Derr-Smith, *The Bride Minaret*
William Greenway, *Everywhere at Once*
Brian Brodeur, *Other Latitudes*
Jeff Gundy, *Spoken among the Trees*
Alison Pelegrin, *Big Muddy River of Stars*
Roger Mitchell, *Half/Mask*
Ashley Capps, *Mistaking the Sea for Green Fields*
Beckian Fritz Goldberg, *The Book of Accident*
Clare Rossini, *Lingo*
Vern Rutsala, *How We Spent Our Time*
Kurt Brown, Meg Kearney, Donna Reis, Estha Weiner, eds.,
Blues for Bill: A Tribute to William Matthews
Sharmila Voorakkara, *Fire Wheel*
Dennis Hinrichsen, *Cage of Water*
Lynn Powell, *The Zones of Paradise*
Roger Mitchell, *Delicate Bait*
William Greenway, *Ascending Order*
George Bilgere, *The Good Kiss*
Melody Lacina, *Private Hunger*
Elton Glaser and William Greenway, eds.,
I Have My Own Song for It: Modern Poems of Ohio
Barry Seiler, *Frozen Falls*
John Minczeski, *Circle Routes*
Susan Yuzna, *Pale Bird, Spouting Fire*
Dennis Hinrichsen, *Detail from* The Garden of Earthly Delights
Marlys West, *Notes for a Late-Blooming Martyr*
Beckian Fritz Goldberg, *Never Be the Horse*
Jeanne E. Clark, *Ohio Blue Tips*
William Greenway, *Simmer Dim*

Barry Seiler, *Black Leaf*

Clare Rossini, *Winter Morning with Crow*

Raeburn Miller, *The Collected Poems of Raeburn Miller*

Susan Yuzna, *Her Slender Dress*

Anita Feng, *Internal Strategies*

Jon Davis, *Scrimmage of Appetite*

William Greenway, *How the Dead Bury the Dead*

Raeburn Miller, *The Comma After Love: Selected Poems of Raeburn Miller*

Barry Seiler, *The Waters of Forgetting*